Sweet Words to God

A Child's Book of Jewish Prayers

RABBI ARNOLD GOODMAN

Illustrated by Daniel Gill

LONGSTREET PRESS
Atlanta

Published by
LONGSTREET PRESS, INC.
2140 Newmarket Parkway
Suite 122
Marietta, GA 30067

Printed in the United States of America

1st printing 2001

Library of Congress Catalog Card Number: 00-112261

ISBN: 1-56352-665-4

Jacket and book design by Burtch Bennett Hunter

Introduction

The Jewish home is called a mikdash me'at—a mini-sanctuary. While the Synagogue experience is treasured and an important component of the Jewish religious life, the home is where early memories are formed and basic attitudes about God, prayer, and community begin to take shape.

Prayer is as central to the home as it is to the Synagogue. Prayer has power. It is a distinct and unique human activity not known to any other form of life. Throughout the ages until this very day, men, women, and children of all religions, creeds, races, in virtually every culture known to us, have articulated some form of prayer. Whether to an invisible God, to an idol, to natural forces, to trees, to totem poles, prayer is a universal form of asking for help, for expressing joy, for creating community.

Through home prayer, parents have a unique opportunity to share spiritual experiences with their children. Praying together can sensitize children to the presence of God in their lives, as well as help them express joy or sadness as they experience both life's ongoing routines and the special moments that can unfold on any day at any time.

Rabbi Arnold Goodman

Table of Contents

Sweet Words to God

Daily Prayers

Before Going to Sleep

שמע ישראל ה׳ אל-הינו ה׳ אחד

Dear God,
Before I close my eyes in sleep and pray for a restful night, I think back to my day. If I have hurt anyone, I ask to be forgiven, and in turn I forgive anyone who may have hurt me. I thank You for parents and family and friends. As I sleep, I hope to feel Your presence. May all my dreams be sweet and may I awaken tomorrow and have a good day. Amen.

Upon Awakening

༄

מודה אני לפניך

Dear God,
Thank you for this new day. I will make it special
by listening to my parents, eating my breakfast
and playing nicely with my friends. Help me
smile and help me make others smile. Amen.

How Healthy I Am

Dear God,
My legs are strong and my eyes are clear.
I feel strong and I bless You, O God,
for helping me stay healthy. Amen.

I'm Ready to Eat

◎◎

המוציא לחם מן הארץ

Dear God,
The food I am about to eat will keep me
healthy and strong. I thank You for helping my
Mommy and Daddy make this meal for me and our
whole family. I am happy for my food and for being
able to share it with the people I love. Amen.

Milk and Cookies – Yum

Dear God,
My milk and cookies are a special treat.
They taste so good and they make me feel very loved.
Why do I always want another one? Amen.

Brushing Up and Brushing Down

Dear God,
Before I get into bed, I brush my teeth up and down. I pray I won't have any cavities. I know that shiny teeth will make my smile look better. I hope I have many reasons to smile a lot. Amen.

Cuddling in Bed
with Mom and Dad

❀

Dear God,
I'm in bed now and I feel so safe when I am with
my Mommy and Daddy. I love to recite my bedtime
prayer and then get a big hug and a goodnight
kiss. They always wish me happy dreams, and
I wish them happy dreams too. Amen.

Special Prayers

When Getting New Clothes

I thank You, O God, who clothes us all. I am blessed to have these nice clothes that make me feel good. I will take care of them and treat them with respect because I know there are children who are not able to have any new clothes, even for special occasions or holidays. I thank You for helping my parents provide me with nice and warm things to wear. Amen.

What a Great Toy

Dear God,
My new toy is fun. I am lucky to have so many toys and games. Most of them are presents not only from Mommy and Daddy but from all the people who love me and want to make sure I am happy. I love them all and someday I will give them all presents. Amen.

It's Scary Outside

꩜

Dear God,
The sky is dark and I can hear the sound the wind is making. The loud noise of the thunder scares me, but it's really exciting when lightning lights up the sky. Storms can pull down trees and make the lights go out and even hurt our house. Keep us safe, God, and make sure that we aren't hurt by the storm. Amen.

Trips Are Fun

꩜

Dear God,
My Mommy says I can take my favorite doll on our trip. We will be away for a long time, maybe even two weeks. Daddy says I will have to be good and not fight with my brother and sister, especially when he is driving. I will try to behave myself. My doll and I want to make sure that our trip is fun. Amen.

No Place Like Home

꩜

Dear God,
It was a fun trip, but after a while I missed being
home with all my toys. I am glad that nobody
touched them while I was gone. Mommy says
it's good to go away and even better to come
home. I love being home with my
family and my toys. Amen.

Happy Birthday to Me

Dear God,

Today is my birthday. I am one year older and my party was lots of fun. I like the presents everyone gave me. I was glad that I could blow out all the candles on my cake and then have everyone sing "Happy Birthday" to me. My birthday will always be a special day, and I hope You will help me have lots of birthdays as I grow up. Amen.

I Love My Pet

Dear God,
I feel lucky to have my pet. I love her, and that's
why I take good care of her and feed her. I have
fun playing with her, and when I am sad she
makes me laugh. I thank you for my pet
and also for all the people who love
me and take care of me. Amen.

My New Baby Sister Is Cute

Dear God,

My new sister is so cute, and I can't wait to hold her. My Mommy tells me that I must be gentle, and I can hardly wait until she grows up and we can play together. I thank you, God, for the present of my new baby sister. Amen.

My New Baby Brother Is Cute

Dear God,

My new brother is so cute, and I can't wait to hold him. My Mommy tells me that I must be gentle, and I can hardly wait until he grows up and we can play together. I thank you, God, for the present of my new baby brother. Amen.

Life Isn't Always Easy

I Feel Sad Today

Dear God,

I feel sad today. Mommy and Daddy say because I didn't behave, they will not let me watch TV or even have my bedtime treat. I promise that I will try to be good and not say or do bad things. Help me keep that promise. Amen.

I Don't Feel Good

Dear God,
I feel sick today. Mommy says I have a fever and must try to rest. I don't like being sick. It's no fun not being able to go outside and play. Thank You for helping me feel good most of the time and make me get better really soon. Amen.

Where Do We Go When We Die?

❀

Dear God,

I wonder where we go after we die. Mommy says we have something inside us that we can't see. She says this is our soul that flies up to You after we die so You can watch over it. Daddy says you take special care of the souls of people who have been good. I will always try to make sure that my soul stays good by listening to my Mommy and Daddy. Amen.

Holidays Are
Lots of fun

Shabbat Is Always Special

@@

בורא פרי הגפן

Dear God,
Shabbat is so special. Mommy lets me set the table
and then we sing together the blessing over the
candles. Later Daddy gives me grape juice in my
special Shabbat cup and then says the blessing over
wine with me. Mommy and Daddy tell me that
Shabbat is special because this is the day You rested
after making the whole world. I love Shabbat. Amen.

A New Beginning

❀❀

לשנה טובה תכתבו

Dear God,
Every day the mailman brings new Rosh Hashanah
cards. Everyone says "Happy New Year" to one
another. Mommy tells me we may have made some
mistakes last year, but today is a new beginning. I
especially like to dip apples in honey as we ask
You for a sweet year. I hope this comes true. Amen.

I Can't Wait to Fast

Dear God,

Today is Yom Kippur when many grown-ups fast, which means they don't eat or drink anything. Mommy says that by not eating we can spend more time thinking about our behavior and ways to make ourselves better people. Before going to Synagogue, we all said, "I'm sorry if I hurt you in any way. Will you forgive me?" And we all forgave each other and hugged and kissed. When I'm older, I will try to fast, and I will always remember to say I'm sorry and kiss all the people I love. Amen.

Trim, Trim, Trim the Sukkah

✆

לישב בסוכה

Dear God,
It's fun to trim the Sukkah. We hang fruit, string
popcorn and draw pictures to decorate the Sukkah.
Sukkot is our Thanksgiving holiday when we remind
ourselves that You protected the Jewish people in the
desert. We don't live in the desert anymore, but we
still want You to care for us and to make sure we
have enough to eat, nice clothes to wear and
warm homes in which to live. Amen.

Turkey Is for Thanksgiving

Dear God,

Turkey and all the side dishes are so good. The whole family was together and it was a lot of fun. Before we ate, Daddy asked us what we were most thankful for. I wasn't sure what my answer was then, but now I have one. I am thankful for my parents, my family, my home, my toys. I feel loved and I love so many people. I hope I will always be able to show my family how much I love them all. Amen.

Eight Nights of Candles and Presents

◎◎

לְהַדְלִיק נֵר שֶׁל חֲנוּכָּה

Dear God,
We light Hanukkah candles for eight nights. It's fun to sing the songs and to give and get presents. Daddy says we have this holiday to remind us that You helped the brave Judah Maccabee and his brothers win a big war and then clean up the Holy Temple in Jerusalem, when a little jar of oil lasted for eight nights. This miracle made good things happen and I hope you will make more miracles today so more good things can happen. Amen.

Purim Costumes Are Fun

חג פורים שמח

Dear God,
I love dressing up for Purim. It's fun to make believe you are someone else who was famous. I always eat too many of the hamantasch cakes. Their three sides remind us of the hat Haman wore. He was very bad. He wanted to kill all the Jews, but You, God, didn't let that happen. That's why we are so happy on this holiday. I hope You will always protect us from bad people. Amen.

Matza and More Matza

❧

הלילה הזה כולו מצה

Dear God,
I'm glad that you sent Moses to free the slaves and
that we have this holiday of Passover. Our whole family
is together at one big table at a big dinner that we call
the Seder. Before we can eat, we will sing songs and tell
stories. The most fun is trying to steal the matza
Daddy hides. When I give it back to him, he gives me
a reward for finding it and for bringing it to him. I
hope I can stay awake until the Seder ends. Amen.

Happy Birthday, Torah

⟋⟍

תורה צוה לנו משה

Dear God,
Birthdays are fun. We don't know when You were
born, but we know the Torah was born on this holiday
of Shavuot. Moses stood on the mountain and You
told him that You wanted the people to be good to
each other. Mommy says that the best present we
can give someone is a big smile and a helping hand.
I hope I can give Torah and You this special
present every day. Amen.